HOW TO
SURVIVE IN
A BAD
ECONOMY

Be The Entrepreneur
You Were Born To Be!

You're Only <u>One Deal</u> <u>Away</u>,
Don't Give Up Now!

10 Steps on How to Win,
With a Combination of
7 Income Streams

ALL I WANT TO KNOW,
ARE YOU READY TO GROW?

HOW TO SURVIVE IN A BAD ECONOMY

Be The Entrepreneur You Were Born To Be!

You're Only <u>One Deal</u> <u>Away</u>, Don't Give Up Now!

ALL I WANT TO KNOW, ARE YOU READY TO GROW?

YOU'RE ONLY ONE (<u>DEAL</u>) AWAY!

From Being Free!

ALL I WANT TO KNOW, ARE YOU READY TO GROW?

Scripture quotations are taken from
The Holy Bible, The King James Version.

Library of Congress Cataloging-in-Publication Data
HOW TO SURVIVE IN A BAD ECONOMY
No. 1-3POR86

Cover design by: Charlie Grant / Touch of Heaven
Book interior design by: Charlie Grant / Fahim Munshi

Printed by: CreateSpace

ISBN-13: 978-1-4499-4122-2
ISBN-10: 1-4499-4122-2

Website: www.cbs-wealthbldg.com
Email: cgrant1996@yahoo.com

ALL I WANT TO KNOW, ARE YOU READY TO GROW?

Comments

"How to Survive in a Bad Economy is a must read for these economic times. It's an excellent resource for learning how to obtain multiple streams of income."

--Dr. Eric Cooper,
Preacher, Speaker & Author of
"Covenant Relationships"

"How To Survive In A Bad Economy is The Answer to the economical woes which are currently ravaging our nation and beyond. Charlie Grant's courage to confront this economic state head on through creating your own way financially is felt with every turn of the page. This is not the book for just keeping your head above water in these trying economical times, rather one which shows how to walk on water and create your financial future your way."

--Matthew C. Horne,
Motivational Speaker &
Author of
"The Universe Is Inviting You In"

"A unique, compelling, quick read. This book includes tips and strategies for all."

--Dr. Eugene Williams, Sr.
Educator, Speaker, Author of
"Words Cross & Across: Word
Search on Barack Obama"

ALL I WANT TO KNOW, ARE YOU READY TO GROW?

Comments

"This is a must read book. With the times of life as they seem to be in today's world, all people need to know how to stay on top of life's circumstances. Enclosed within these pages are key ingredients to making a healthier lifestyle for you and your family. However, you must make the commitment to read and apply the principles of the book in order for them to manifest. You will be glad that you invested in this treasure of information that will help you to obtain your goals to a solid lifestyle. Read and enjoy"

--Pastor's Morgan,
Healing Hands Ministries,
& Author's of
"Seven Steps To
Keeping Intimacy
After You Say I Do"

"After reading **"How To Survive In a BAD Economy"**. The book touched my heart deeply. This book is a prescription to heal you from a BAD Economy or any other drought that you are going through in _LIFE_. **"How To Survive In a BAD Economy"** is a tool that we can use to refurbish our present condition. The insight that I absorbed from this book was that we can Re-Invent ourselves at any point of our lives. How To Survive In A BAD Economy is **_timeless._**"

--Ulysses Cooper,
The Real Estate Tycoon

ALL I WANT TO KNOW, ARE YOU READY TO GROW?

Comments

"One *MUST* use Charlie Grant's information and advice at this pivotal time in our lives. The book provides daily and long term strategies on "How to survive in a bad economy". The title could have easily read "...survive and excel...""

--Dr. Daryl Stone,
          Professor,
          Bowie State University

ALL I WANT TO KNOW, ARE YOU READY TO GROW?

ACKNOWLEDGMENTS

To <u>Jesus</u> who is the Christ who is first and foremost in my life. Lord, I'm so very thankful and blessed, for your spirit that leads me and guides me on this journey called life, and for placing on my heart the call to help people by way of motivation and education.

To my <u>mother</u> who's shown me more love than I could ever asked for. Who's always been in my corner. Who has sacrificed so much and paid a price so that I could be where I am, at this point in my life. Momma, I love you with all my heart.

To my <u>family,</u> whom I love so very much. Thanks for all your patience, love, and support. And for motivating and cooperating with my busy schedule and dreams. Kids, you inspire me everyday to never quit until we reach the top. You're the greatest. You will be blessed!

To my <u>brothers and sister</u>, I thank you for your love and support. Continue to stay focused on your dreams. And the Lord God will bless you.

ALL I WANT TO KNOW, ARE YOU READY TO GROW?

ACKNOWLEDGMENTS

To my great friends <u>Les Brown</u>, <u>Willie Jolley</u>, <u>George Fraser</u>, <u>Rodney Green,</u> and <u>Reginald Pastuer</u>. You all have inspired me in the mist of my pain, my purpose, and my passion. I'm very grateful for your gift and positive mindset.

To <u>Pastor Robert G. Childs</u>, my spiritual father, my pastor, my mentor, and my friend, who has deposited so much into my life spiritually and mentally. I could never repay you for that, Doc. You are such a spiritual giant and a true man of God. Thanks so very much for guiding me on my spiritual journey, and for giving me the chance to find my purpose and passion in life.

To <u>Pastor Grainger and Joann Browning</u>, you have been a great inspiration in my life over the last few years. Thanks for keeping me on fire, when I thought my pilot was a little low. Also, I thank God for you and your powerful ministry, along with instilling in me that the best is yet to come.

ALL I WANT TO KNOW, ARE YOU READY TO GROW?

ACKNOWLEDGMENTS

To <u>Ivey J. Stokes, Dr. James Boone, Dr. Harrison Foyee, and Damon Moates</u>, I would like to thank you guys for all of your wisdom, knowledge, and friendship. You guys have empowered me with more knowledge than any school I've ever been to, including college. I'm so very grateful to you all.

To all my <u>business partners</u> and <u>team members</u> at <u>CBS Institute For Learning</u>, <u>HBBRP</u>, <u>Young Entrepreneurship Program</u>, <u>Business Management Money Group</u>, <u>Economic Empowerment Dream Team, and Men Of Purpose;</u> thanks for your faithfulness and your desire to win and succeed. You're like pure gold.

To my <u>students</u>, you are the joy and the desire that continues to keep me on this wonderful journey to motivate and educate one billion men and women and to help thousands of people become financially free. Also, to impact, inspire, educate, and support young people all across this country. You are awesome!

ALL I WANT TO KNOW, ARE YOU READY TO GROW?

TABLE OF <u>CONTENTS</u>

Part 1 (10 Ways To Win)

ALL I WANT TO KNOW, ARE YOU READY TO GROW?

TABLE OF <u>CONTENTS</u>

Part 2 (-7 Streams Of Income-)

ALL I WANT TO KNOW, ARE YOU READY TO GROW?

TABLE OF
CONTENTS

ALL I WANT TO KNOW,
ARE YOU READY TO GROW?

WELCOME

Hello, I'm Charlie Grant, speaker, trainer, author, founder, and CEO of CBS Institute for Learning, where information is power.

I welcome you this day; you are on your way to living your best life ever and learning; how to survive in a bad economy.

*My goals and objectives are to motivate and educate you. Also, to give you life-changing strategies and tips that will help you to survive in any economy. In this economy you must overcome your challenges and be able to bounce back. You're a **survivor**!*

ALL I WANT TO KNOW, ARE YOU READY TO GROW?

WELCOME / PRAYER

Lord I pray this book might motivate, might cultivate, might stimulate, might educate, build desire, and inspire men and women, boys and girls, so that one day, successfully, they will be able to retire.

And to understand how to survive in a bad economy, first they must take cover under the power and the high tower of the Almighty.

ALL I WANT TO KNOW, ARE YOU READY TO GROW?

GIVING HONOR

First of all, I would like to give honor where honor is due: to the Great Eloheim, El-Shaddai, Jehovah-Nissi, Jehovah-Jireh my provider.

To the God of Abraham, Isaac and Jacob. To the one who stepped out onto nothing reached into nowhere, and pulled all of this into existence.

To the one who designed my destiny before my father and mother knew each other, to the prince of peace, rock of ages, bread of life, to the sweet rose of Sharon, Mary's baby, John's baptismal candidate, Lazarus grave robber, Nelson Mandela's

ALL I WANT TO KNOW, ARE YOU READY TO GROW?

GIVING HONOR

company keeper, Martin Luther King's dream sender, my grandmother's leaning post, my granddaddy's walking stick, my bridge over troubled waters, my heavy load lightener, my dark day brightener, my everything and my all and all.

First of all, I would like to give honor to Jesus who is the Christ, who is first and foremost in my life.

ALL I WANT TO KNOW, ARE YOU READY TO GROW?

INTRODUCTION

How do you survive in a bad economy? Become the entrepreneur you were born to be! I realize that not everyone will become the entrepreneur they were born to be, but I truly believe the key to surviving in this economy is to utilize your gifts and talents, to obtain revenue streams in your own business. Multiple cash flow streams are critical in a bad economy. In this book you will find strategies, tips, and instructions on how to survive in any economy for the entrepreneur and for the person who's still working a 9 to 5. Allow me to share some of my experiences. Before I became an entrepreneur, I utilized my college degree in computer science to obtain

ALL I WANT TO KNOW, ARE YOU READY TO GROW?

INTRODUCTION

several great career opportunities with major corporations, like US Air, Marriott, MCI, UNISYS (Sperry/Univac), EDS Electronic Data Systems, Perot Systems, Standard Federal Bank, Freddie Mac, Rail Inc. etc. I made a good six figure income in computers. I worked with computers for more than 20 years, designing and developing software, utilizing PCs and Mainframes.

I was laid off 3 times, mostly based on yearly budgets. That led me to do some research. I found that most companies do a budget every year from October through January meaning that one

ALL I WANT TO KNOW, ARE YOU READY TO GROW?

INTRODUCTION

year you or I just might not be in the budget. Also, I found that after working a job for forty (40) years, only about 4 out of every 100 people can retire without depending on family, friends or the government. Meaning, that most people retire broke or below their means after forty (40) years of service. So they retire, only to go back to doing something part-time, which turns into another fulltime job until age 75. What kind of life is that?

I realized after doing my research that working a job would just pay the bills and was not the answer to financial freedom. Also, that I had no control over budget

ALL I WANT TO KNOW, ARE YOU READY TO GROW?

INTRODUCTION

cuts. Along, with a path that was most traveled, but not successful by the age of 65. At that point, it was time to take control of my destiny. So, I walked out on a six-figure income, never to look back again.

Yes, I left Corporate America to pursue what the Lord had called and purposed me to do. I stepped out on faith and the rest is history. I always had a burning desire to run my own company. At this point I'm not trying to impress you, but to inspire you. Once again, not to impress you but to impress upon you, that you can

ALL I WANT TO KNOW, ARE YOU READY TO GROW?

INTRODUCTION

do it too, or a lot more. Most of you are already there and much further.

When I became an entrepreneur I made a six-figure income 2 times, first with computer contracts, and second by opening a learning institute. My third entrepreneurial venture was investing and teaching real estate, where I created a seven (7) figure net worth. Ladies and gentlemen, I should have cashed out before the big bomb. But I wanted to live my life like it was golden, so I continued to invest and reinvest to take that seven (7) figure to eight (8) figures. Not trying to be greedy, but to obtain financial

ALL I WANT TO KNOW, ARE YOU READY TO GROW?

INTRODUCTION

resources to send my kids to college, create financial freedom, and to be able to bless people who are in need.

I don't think Oprah Winfrey or Donald Trump would have cashed out either!

I invested in all kinds of real estate, single-family homes, condos, water front property, golf course community properties, etc.

I lived in almost a 7,000 square-foot gated home with a total of five cars in the garage and drive way, within a golf course country club community.

ALL I WANT TO KNOW, ARE YOU READY TO GROW?

INTRODUCTION

With the real estate bomb it felt like I lost almost everything overnight! But, I never stop moving and shaking although my cash flow, began to get low and slow.

I continued to motivate and educate. Just with a much smaller budget. My faith in Jesus Christ pulled me through that test, along with my good friend Willie Jolley's, book; a setback is a setup for a comeback and my good friend Les Brown's book; it's not over until I win.

I always knew if you held the recipe and had the right ingredients you could get it all back and a lot more.

ALL I WANT TO KNOW, ARE YOU READY TO GROW?

INTRODUCTION

Most of the time, double for your trouble. You learn so much from your first experience that the next time around you're so much more: wiser, skillful, and knowledgeable.

In life, you must be able to take a punch! Even if you get knock down, you must be able to get back up off the canvas of life and continue to throw punches. Sooner or later you're going to hit your target and WIN!

Note: Ladies and gentlemen, when you're sick and tired of being sick and tired and ready to throw in the towel... Even on your darkest night, when you're mad and

ALL I WANT TO KNOW, ARE YOU READY TO GROW?

INTRODUCTION

ready to fight... And when, you can't find anyone to help, on your left or your right.

This book will send you on a wonderful flight that will make everything all right! It's based on motivation and education, which produces relaxation. When your finances are great and you're at the train station ready to take a well deserved vacation.

Get ready to change your life in the next 90 days!

ALL I WANT TO KNOW, ARE YOU READY TO GROW?

You're Only One (<u>Deal</u>) Away!

How to survive in a bad economy?

Making the right deal can set you free in a bad economy!

**ALL I WANT TO KNOW,
ARE YOU READY TO GROW?**

<u>ONE</u> DEAL AWAY !

YOU'RE ONLY:

ONE IDEA

ONE PHONE CALL

ONE EMAIL

ONE FAX

ONE CONTRACT

ONE LOAN

ONE SIGNATURE

ONE EVENT

ONE REFERRAL

ONE INVENTION

**ALL I WANT TO KNOW,
ARE YOU READY TO GROW?**

<u>ONE</u> DEAL AWAY!

ONE RELATIONSHIP

ONE PRAYER

ONE DANCE

ONE KNOCKOUT

ONE BREAK

ONE HAND SHAKE

ONE BOOK

ONE OPPORTUNITY

AWAY FROM BEING
FREE!

ALL I WANT TO KNOW,
ARE YOU READY TO GROW?

ONE DEAL AWAY!
Example # 1:
Buying a business,
like a Laundromat

IF YOU MAKE $40,000.00 A YEAR ON YOUR JOB!

When you buy a $300,000.00 Laundromat, that returns 20% on your investment each year, you would receive $60,000.00. This return would be after all expenses and taxes have been paid, and you would not work the business. You would oversee the business system from your home or on the beach, once a month. This $60,000.00 would replace your $40,000.00 on your job. At this point you could fire your boss.

Based on this one deal !

ALL I WANT TO KNOW, ARE YOU READY TO GROW?

ONE DEAL AWAY!
Example # 2:
Buying Commercial Real Estate, like a 50-unit Apt. Bldg.

IF YOU MAKE $75,000.00 A YEAR ON YOUR JOB!

If you bought a $1,500,000.00 apartment building, that returned 5% on your investment each year. Based on most apartments, on average the return is about 4% - 10%. Then you would have a total of $75,000.00 each year. This return would be after all expenses and taxes have been paid, and you would not work the business. You would oversee the business system from your home or on the beach, once a month, and maintain property managers that would take care of the building rents and maintenance. At this point you could fire your boss.

Based on this one deal!

ALL I WANT TO KNOW, ARE YOU READY TO GROW?

31

ONE DEAL AWAY!

Example # 3:
Buying a business, like a Hotel

IF YOUR FAMILY OF **FOUR** MAKE $50,000.00
EACH, WHICH WOULD BE A TOTAL OF
$200,000.00 A YEAR AT THEIR JOBS.

If they came together and bought a $2,000,000.00
hotel that returned 10% on their investment each
year, then they would have a total of $200,000.00
each year, divided by **four** people. Each one of them
would receive $50,000.00. This return would be after
all expenses and taxes have been paid, and they
would not work the business. They would oversee the
business system from their homes or on the beach,
once a month, and maintain the same employee's that
were there when they bought the Hotel.
At that point each one of them could fire their bosses.

Based on _this one deal_ !

ALL I WANT TO KNOW,
ARE YOU READY TO GROW?

AUTO UNIVERSITY

The way to obtain
a free degree!

How to survive in a bad economy? A good education can open up opportunities to set you free in a bad economy.

You can obtain motivational and educational College knowledge, right from the comfort of your own vehicle. Get your certificate today.

Utilize time spent in your vehicle wisely, by listening to motivational and educational materials. A perfect method to enhance and advance your education. "This is a great way to prevent a break-down"!

The motivation continues to build self-esteem and the education helps you to fulfill the dream!

There are Universities in your state, city, or town; and then there's Universities all around.

ALL I WANT TO KNOW, ARE YOU READY TO GROW?

AUTO UNIVERSITY

Even, there are online college course programs.

*But, you're in your car 5-7 days a week,
on average two hours per day.*

**So what are you waiting for?
Start working on your degree today.
Purchase something
motivational and educational.**

CDs, DVDs, Books, and Courses

www.cbs-wealthbldg.com

THE ONLY (MBA) YOU NEED IS A (M)ajor (B)ank (A)ccount!

ALL I WANT TO KNOW, ARE YOU READY TO GROW?

MOTIVATION And EDUCATION

THE PERFECT COMBINATION!

Motivation and Education, are the keys for success!

It's like gasoline to a car,
It's like water to a flower,
It's like food to the body,
It's like cash in a bad economy
You've got to have it!

ALL I WANT TO KNOW, ARE YOU READY TO GROW?

MOTIVATION And EDUCATION

It's all about the combination, motivation, and education. It's just like opening up a vault or safe, you must have the correct combination.

Like baking a cake you must know the recipe and have the correct ingredients.

You must find your purpose and passion, which will unlock the magical door to a great outpour of financial revenues like never before.

ALL I WANT TO KNOW, ARE YOU READY TO GROW?

Be The Entrepreneur You Were Born To Be!

Business woman or man, step out on faith, get out of the gate, before it's too late. It's time to take a stand. God has you in his hand. If you fall, he will catch you when you land!

Do what you showed up on the planet to do, and God will bless you and your crew.

Take the time to find out what your assignment is, what you have been called to do, and then pursue. It's on you; what will you do?

You must be willing to reinvent yourself everyday!

ALL I WANT TO KNOW, ARE YOU READY TO GROW?

Be The Entrepreneur You Were Born To Be!

Do what comes natural to you; that you can't help but to do, and allow it to bring you revenue!

I realized that one solution, to surviving in a bad economy would be, find a problem and then solve it (through business!)

"It Only Takes a Minute to Change Your Life"
By: Willie Jolley

ALL I WANT TO KNOW, ARE YOU READY TO GROW?

Part One

10 Ways
To Win

**ALL I WANT TO KNOW,
ARE YOU READY TO GROW?**

TEN WAYS TO WIN

1. Cut Your Expenses ASAP

Put your pride to the side; it's not the time to worry about what other people will say or think about you based on your new situation and lack of revenue.

Give back that stolen vehicle if you have not paid your car note in the last three months or been given an extension.

You might have to downsize your home.

Stop eating out every day or night.

Stop spoiling the kids and show tough love; quit buying them everything.

You might have to start wearing the same outfit more than once, cut back on the cleaners and buying new clothes.

ALL I WANT TO KNOW, ARE YOU READY TO GROW?

TEN WAYS TO WIN

Have one mate (HA, HA, HA) then you will only have to pay for one date and one plate.

Create three financial statements: an income statement, a balance sheet, and a net worth statement to see where you are financially.

Raise your exemptions on your job.

Take time to remove all the distractions out of your life (people, devices, etc.).

Find out what type of public assistance programs you qualify for (food, unemployment, insurance, etc.)

Work on your credit to obtain low rates. And no money down deals!

Check with your car dealer to see if you can use regular gas.

ALL I WANT TO KNOW, ARE YOU READY TO GROW?

TEN WAYS TO WIN

Notes:

_____

_____

_____

_____

_____

_____

_____

_____

_____

_____

ALL I WANT TO KNOW, ARE YOU READY TO GROW?

TEN WAYS TO WIN

Strategies:

_____

_____

_____

_____

_____

_____

_____

_____

_____

**ALL I WANT TO KNOW,
ARE YOU READY TO GROW?**

TEN WAYS TO WIN

2. Focus on Multiple Streams of Income!

When one stream dries up, there should be another stream ready to open up! Some times God closes one door, because he's ready to open **up a double door! A door that will close no more!**

T.D. Jakes, once said, "Every gift and talent the LORD blesses you with should be a stream of income."

Work on several ways to obtain residual income, to make money while you're eating and sleeping.

It's time to take some risk. It's time for hit or miss. It's time to think out of the box. It's time to create gold like Fort Knox!

ALL I WANT TO KNOW, ARE YOU READY TO GROW?

TEN WAYS TO WIN

Never allow your family's survival to be based on one income stream or a job.

Multiple streams of cash flow are critical for survival!

You must have at least <u>three (3) streams of income</u> or more. If not, you are risking everything. In a bad economy, if one stream shuts down, that stream could cause a domino effect on the second stream to be plowed down. That would only leave you with the third stream.

ALL I WANT TO KNOW, ARE YOU READY TO GROW?

TEN WAYS TO WIN

Notes:

_____

_____

_____

_____

_____

_____

_____

_____

_____

_____

**ALL I WANT TO KNOW,
ARE YOU READY TO GROW?**

TEN WAYS TO WIN

Strategies:

_____

_____

_____

_____

_____

_____

_____

_____

_____

_____

ALL I WANT TO KNOW, ARE YOU READY TO GROW?

TEN WAYS TO WIN

3. Finding Your Purpose And Passion

Time to cash in on your passion!

It's time to <u>step</u> into your greatness

If you don't use it, and if you abuse it, you just might lose it!

My favorite book states that your gift will make room for you at the top!

This is the greatest calling on your life! Weather you choose to accept it or reject it, if you choose not to accept your assignment, you might walk in darkness on many occasions or have a void in your life.

Because, what you love to do, what you've been called to do, what you've been born to do, is a part of you. It's all up to you! What will you do?

ALL I WANT TO KNOW, ARE YOU READY TO GROW?

TEN WAYS TO WIN

Folks, Now Is The Time! to show up and show out. Now is the time to see what you're all about.

Now, is the time to show why you showed up on the planet. Now is the time to see if your gift will make money for you like a magnet.

Now is the time to bust a move! Now is the time to get into your groove, your element.

Now is the time to leave a mark that cannot be erased because the blessing that you have is right in your face.

Now is the time to get out of that same space, that same place; so that you can obtain increase.

Now is the time to find out that payday is on the way, so don't forget to pray!

Now, is the time not tonight, not tomorrow, not next week, but now. Don't waste another moment; life is not promised.

ALL I WANT TO KNOW, ARE YOU READY TO GROW?

TEN WAYS TO WIN

My pastor, Robert G. Childs of Berean Baptist Church in Washington, DC. Holy Ghost fire, baptized, preaching, teaching, anointed & appointed man of God. College professor, play writer, musician & songbird: a giant of a man with many gifts and talents. But yet a true man of God, with a strong love for the people of this world. He was the greatest influence in my life, helping me to find my purpose and passion.   (Church Phone # 202-829-8454)

Allow me to take a quick detour!

Over 20 years ago, Pastor Robert G. Childs started a young men's group. Within the community of N.W. Washington, DC., yours truly, Charlie Grant, was a part of that group. We had rap sessions, we read from positive study books and from the Bible. We were always asked, if we had used any drugs, to read and pray at each session. This meant that we had to be accountable to somebody. One day after praying, Pastor asked me to do the morning prayer, on youth day. I said no way. I was shocked, due that I stuttered when I spoke, and I did not like to talk in front of

ALL I WANT TO KNOW,
ARE YOU READY TO GROW?

TEN WAYS TO WIN

crowds. But, he saw something in me that I did not see in myself. I was so afraid I started not to show up for church that Sunday. But, I thought about it; with me living next door to the church, he would see me anyway. So I prayed, to my surprise I did not stutter not one time. This started to give me a little confidence in myself. I always wanted to speak like Pastor Childs, who was a great orator. After that he gave me chance after chance after chance to be a part of several church programs where I had to speak, pray, act or read in front of lots of people. Not only did this increase my spiritual growth, it allowed me to overcome my biggest fear, speaking in front of people, because of my stuttering. Through many people telling me how great I had done or praising me when I prayed or spoke, in church or out of church, this allowed me to see that this was my true gift (speaking!) along with a test in church that showed the same gift.

He also gave me assignments to read certain books and lesson plans on the word of God. One book

ALL I WANT TO KNOW, ARE YOU READY TO GROW?

TEN WAYS TO WIN

assignment was very special, it changed my life. When he had me to read the book, " The Greatest Salesman In The World" by OG MANDINO. That book really opened my eyes and motivated me to be great. That, youth program experience, helped to inspire me to start my own youth group. To share, give back and assist like what was given unto me by Pastor Robert Childs.

Doc, I'm very grateful; words cannot express how thankful I am for your faithfulness and for taking the time to bless a young man like me!

(That's True Ministry!)

ALL I WANT TO KNOW, ARE YOU READY TO GROW?

TEN WAYS TO WIN

Notes:

_____

_____

_____

_____

_____

_____

_____

_____

_____

_____

ALL I WANT TO KNOW,
ARE YOU READY TO GROW?

TEN WAYS TO WIN

Strategies:

_____

_____

_____

_____

_____

_____

_____

_____

_____

_____

**ALL I WANT TO KNOW,
ARE YOU READY TO GROW?**

TEN WAYS TO WIN

4. Start Your Own Business

A. *Choose your product or service. It should line up with your purpose and passion.*
B. *Develop a business name*
C. *Develop a business plan*
D. *Get your business registered*
E. *Get a license if needed*
F. *Get your EIN #*
G. *Find financing*
H. *Get a bank account*
I. *Develop a web-site*
J. *Get started today!*

ALL I WANT TO KNOW, ARE YOU READY TO GROW?

TEN WAYS TO WIN

Start your business today, you're only a prayer away, woman or man, how long have you ran, it's time for your business plan, it's time to take a stand, you're in demand!

ALL I WANT TO KNOW, ARE YOU READY TO GROW?

TEN WAYS TO WIN

Notes:

_____

_____

_____

_____

_____

_____

_____

_____

_____

_____

_____

**ALL I WANT TO KNOW,
ARE YOU READY TO GROW?**

TEN WAYS TO WIN

Strategies:

_____

_____

_____

_____

_____

_____

_____

_____

_____

_____

**ALL I WANT TO KNOW,
ARE YOU READY TO GROW?**

TEN WAYS TO WIN

5. It's Not Going To Be Easy

Friends are going to talk about you. Your family will ask why you left that good government job. People are going to think you're crazy. Sometimes you're going to think you're crazy!

It's not going to be easy. Business can be up or down: You can be making $30-$40 thousand dollars a month & go to making $10 thousand over-night. I know because it happened to me. Creditors calling your home, your children pick up the phone, my daddy says he isn't home. The bank won't give you the loan.

It's not going to be easy. You're going to lose some friends, maybe family; you're going to have to check who you hang with!

There are two (2) types of relationships; NURTURING and then there's TOXIC.

ALL I WANT TO KNOW, ARE YOU READY TO GROW?

TEN WAYS TO WIN

Nurturing relationships are when people hold you accountable, they check you, they push you, they encourage you, they inspire you, they bring the best out of you, they want the best for you!

Toxic relationships are when people never listen to you, they are always negative, it's always your fault, they always want to argue, they always bring up your mistakes, they are undercover player haters.(**They smile in your face, when all the time they want to take your place back stabbers.**)

Nurturing and Toxic Relationships
(by: Les Brown)

It's not going to be easy;
stop spending major time with minor people!
(by: George Fraser)

It's not going to be easy; you might have to borrow some money, when cash gets funny.

ALL I WANT TO KNOW, ARE YOU READY TO GROW?

TEN WAYS TO WIN

Notes:

_____

_____

_____

_____

_____

_____

_____

_____

_____

ALL I WANT TO KNOW,
ARE YOU READY TO GROW?

TEN WAYS TO WIN

Strategies:

_____

_____

_____

_____

_____

_____

_____

_____

_____

_____

**ALL I WANT TO KNOW,
ARE YOU READY TO GROW?**

TEN WAYS TO WIN

6. You Can Never Quit

Donald Trump's father told him a story about his friend, who loved soda. He had developed a new soda business. First he called it Second Up, then Third Up, then Fourth Up, then he stopped at Fifth Up, he came back for Six Up, and then he quit. Then, somebody came out the next year with Seven Up, and it BLEW UP!

One man said failure is the price tag for success! You can never quit!

You can never throw in the towel!

It's not over until the fat lady sings! (Les Brown would say, **it's not over until I win!**) **Several years ago, I was** playing basketball, with my son Joshua Grant. At the time Joshua was only 10 years old. I beat him 7 straight games.

ALL I WANT TO KNOW, ARE YOU READY TO GROW?

TEN WAYS TO WIN

Then I stretched and said, "Dad's a little tired now. I think I'm going to go in to get some work done." Little Joshua jumped up in my face, "Dad", "Dad!" [**It's not over until I win!**] He had the eye of the tiger!

So we began to play several more games. Finally little Joshua won a game. Then he stretched and said, "Dad, I'm a little tired now, I think I'm going to go on in and (play a video game)."

It dawned on me at that point that we, too, must be like the Joshua Grant's of the world, **We must have the eye of the tiger. When people tell you no, no, no, no! And when life starts knocking you down, again and again and again, Jump back up and say it's not over until I WIN! (ohhhhhhh it's not over yet!)**

ALL I WANT TO KNOW, ARE YOU READY TO GROW?

TEN WAYS TO WIN

It's not over until the Lord blesses you and me!
It's not over until we are financially free, ohhhhhhh
It's not over yet!
It's not over until my kids graduate and I can
celebrate! It's not over yet!

In business sometimes it's a mess, but it's nothing but a test, so do your due diligence & preparation and you shall soar above the rest!

In business you can't quit , you can't split, you can't run out on it, you got to be legit, so step up to the plate & get a hit.

ALL I WANT TO KNOW, ARE YOU READY TO GROW?

TEN WAYS TO WIN

Notes:

_____

_____

_____

_____

_____

_____

_____

_____

_____

ALL I WANT TO KNOW,
ARE YOU READY TO GROW?

TEN WAYS TO WIN

Strategies:

_____

_____

_____

_____

_____

_____

_____

_____

_____

**ALL I WANT TO KNOW,
ARE YOU READY TO GROW?**

TEN WAYS TO WIN

7. You Must Be Able To Comeback

You must be able to comeback bigger and better stronger than ever.
The key is, can you endure to stormy weather?

TYLER PERRY (COMEBACK),
OPRAH WINFREY (COMEBACK),
T.D. JAKES (COMEBACK),
LES BROWN (COMEBACK),
MICHAEL JORDAN (COMEBACK),
BOB JOHNSON (COMEBACK),
NELSON MANDELA (COMEBACK)

If Bobby Brown can comeback, then I know you can comeback!
Because it's your prerogative!

Donnie McClurkin, the great gospel singer, sang the song "We Fall Down". But, we get up! (You can never stay down!)

ALL I WANT TO KNOW, ARE YOU READY TO GROW?

TEN WAYS TO WIN

Notes:

_____

_____

_____

_____

_____

_____

_____

_____

_____

**ALL I WANT TO KNOW,
ARE YOU READY TO GROW?**

TEN WAYS TO WIN

Strategies:

_____

_____

_____

_____

_____

_____

_____

_____

_____

_____

**ALL I WANT TO KNOW,
ARE YOU READY TO GROW?**

TEN WAYS TO WIN

8. You Must Invest In Yourself

Les Brown, (Speaker, Trainer & Author)
People invest more in entertainment than empowerment!

**Robert Kiyosaki, (Author Rich Dad, Poor Dad)
There are three types of education:
Academic, Professional & Financial!**

**(The most important education is,
FINANCIAL!)**

**WHEN WAS THE LAST TIME YOU INVESTED
IN YOUR FINANCIAL EDUCATION?**

Tell yourself, "Put your money where your mouth is!" Ask the question, when was the last time you bought a book to enhance your knowledge?

**When was the last time you took a class besides high school or college? Invest in your mind!
Read one to two books a month!**

ALL I WANT TO KNOW, ARE YOU READY TO GROW?

TEN WAYS TO WIN

Notes:

_____

_____

_____

_____

_____

_____

_____

_____

_____

**ALL I WANT TO KNOW,
ARE YOU READY TO GROW?**

TEN WAYS TO WIN

Strategies:

_____

_____

_____

_____

_____

_____

_____

_____

_____

ALL I WANT TO KNOW,
ARE YOU READY TO GROW?

TEN WAYS TO WIN

9. You Must Have A Team

It takes a team to fulfill the dream!
Teamwork makes the dream work!

A great man wrote, individuals win games,
teams win championships! It's a lonely road
to the top without a team. Don't leave home
without one.

Also, you need an all-star coaching staff!
Even Michael Jordan had a coach, Phil
Jackson. Tiger Woods had his father; Serena
& Venus had their dad also. Even Muhammad
Ali had Angelo Dundee!

**Get some coaching, based on your passion.
Information without application leads to
frustration! We all need someone to show
us how to apply our knowledge in this
game call life. (*We all need a coach in life*!)**

ALL I WANT TO KNOW,
ARE YOU READY TO GROW?

TEN WAYS TO WIN

Notes:

_____

_____

_____

_____

_____

_____

_____

_____

_____

_____

ALL I WANT TO KNOW,
ARE YOU READY TO GROW?

TEN WAYS TO WIN

Strategies:

_____

_____

_____

_____

_____

_____

_____

_____

_____

ALL I WANT TO KNOW, ARE YOU READY TO GROW?

TEN WAYS TO WIN

10. You Must Be Willing To Give Back

My way of giving back was to launch a youth program, called YEP (Young Entrepreneur Program). I developed this program based, on my passion for young people and the love of entrepreneurship. We focus on helping young people to utilize their gifts and talents. We also, teach them about business, how to develop business plans, finances, dressing for success and product development. Our foundational keys that we share with our youth are self-esteem, character, and life skills.

We've taken them on trips to New York City to find out how business is really run on Wall Street. This kind of experience allows them to understand that they to can obtain a legal business and still make money vs. selling drugs.

ALL I WANT TO KNOW, ARE YOU READY TO GROW?

TEN WAYS TO WIN

*[**If you would like to donate your time, talent or resources, please review our contact information in the back of the book.**]*
(thanks!)

These days we must find a way to capture our young people's attention, to obtain a chance to share with them. Their attention span is very short.

One of the techniques we utilize is a form of speech that they can identify with. Such as:

Young people, it's time to rise up,
it's time to mount up,
it's time to get up,
it's time to wake up!
its time to get your grades up,
get your pants up,
it's time to change your
product,
young lady it's time to wise up
it's time to cover up!

ALL I WANT TO KNOW, ARE YOU READY TO GROW?

TEN WAYS TO WIN

Young people, its time to dress for success,
its time to dress like a prospect,
opposed to a suspect, so that
you can come correct, with
respect, so that one day, you
will qualify for the big pay
check!

Young people, you're not generation X; you're
generation next. You are not at
risk or hopeless, you too can
be on the dean's list. You just
must focus, pursue and persist
and then you won't miss and
you will have success just
like this >> $$$$$.

Young people, you got to stay in school that's
the golden rule, don't be no
fool, because we need you.
Because you've got to get to
college to obtain the

ALL I WANT TO KNOW,
ARE YOU READY TO GROW?

TEN WAYS TO WIN

knowledge, to keep the money
in your wallet.

Young people, tell the world, your (**Bet
Version**); I'm a business owner,
I put a product on yah, I buy
them at wholesale, sell them at
retail, I'm the King of Sales.

Young people, say we are admired to be
inspired, to be motivated,
dedicated and educated;
for any task entrepreneur
related, we won't hesitate,
debate or procrastinate, because
it might be too late on another
date.

ALL I WANT TO KNOW,
ARE YOU READY TO GROW?

TEN WAYS TO WIN

Notes:

_____

_____

_____

_____

_____

_____

_____

_____

_____

_____

ALL I WANT TO KNOW,
ARE YOU READY TO GROW?

TEN WAYS TO WIN

Strategies:

_____

_____

_____

_____

_____

_____

_____

_____

ALL I WANT TO KNOW,
ARE YOU READY TO GROW?

Take Action.

Get started with your very own,
How To Survive In A Bad Economy
Coach Today!

Everyone needs a coach in life.
Working with a coach will help you
to begin a new, successful chapter in
your life. *"Don't waste another
moment."*

Learn how to profit in the good
times <u>and</u> the bad times.

It's time to be the successful person
you were born to be!
_____+++_____
CBS Institute For Learning
*9900-E Greenbelt Rd,
Suite 243
Lanham, MD 20706*
Contact Us Today!
Website: www.cbs-wealthbldg.com
Email: cgrant1996@yahoo.com
_____+++_____

ALL I WANT TO KNOW,
ARE YOU READY TO GROW?

Part Two

7 Streams Of Income

ALL I WANT TO KNOW, ARE YOU READY TO GROW?

STREAMS OF INCOME

REAL ESTATE

Income Stream #1:
Real Estate

Real estate is a great asset. More people have gotten wealthy from real estate than any other asset. You have a great chance to create income from real estate because of OPM: "Other Peoples Money." Even in a bad economy. Take note, if you went to the bank to borrow a hundred thousand dollars to invest in the stock market most likely they'd tell you no. If you went to the bank to borrow a hundred

---

When God gives you a vision he makes provision.

ALL I WANT TO KNOW, ARE YOU READY TO GROW?

STREAMS OF INCOME

REAL ESTATE

thousand dollars to start up a new business they'll take you through all kinds of red tape, but if you ask the bank to borrow a hundred thousand dollars to buy some real estate, they'll just say, "Let's take a look at your credit." That's why real estates is so great; I used to say, "I have date with a steak and a plate and can't be late, but now I'm talking real estate."

Invest in your mind: if you don't this is a crime, meaning you will trade a dollar for a dime.

ALL I WANT TO KNOW, ARE YOU READY TO GROW?

STREAMS OF INCOME

*But thou shalt remember the Lord thy God:
for it is he that giveth thee power to get wealth.
Deuteronomy 8:18*

REAL ESTATE

*There are two basic real estate markets, a
buyer's market and a seller's market.*

1. *A buyer's market
   A buyer's market is normally when there
   is an overflow of properties or when
   there is more supply than demand.
   The prices are very low based on
   overflow.*

*Your attitude determines your altitude: your
preparation shall determine your destination.*

ALL I WANT TO KNOW,
ARE YOU READY TO GROW?

87

STREAMS OF INCOME

Happy is the man that findeth wisdom, and the man that getteth understanding. Proverbs 3:13

REAL ESTATE

2. *A seller's market*
   A seller's market is when there is a shortage of supply and great demand for properties.
   The prices are high based on a lack of supply.

God wants you to create wealth, so don't lay your gifts and talents up on a shelf: just be yourself and he'll be there to surely help.

ALL I WANT TO KNOW, ARE YOU READY TO GROW?

STREAMS OF INCOME

REAL ESTATE

Let's talk about 3 types of loans. One would be a Conventional Loan, next would be a VA Veterans Administration Loan and third would be FHA Federal Housing Authority Loan. There are also five major cost involved with buying real estate.

#1 Earnest Money Deposit

#3 Homeowner Insurance

#2 Appraisal Fee

#4 Closing Costs

#5 Down Payment

When you come to CBS Academy, you'll know your strategy like your anatomy.

ALL I WANT TO KNOW, ARE YOU READY TO GROW?

STREAMS OF INCOME

REAL ESTATE

There are a lot of ways to make money in real-estate as an investor, let's talk about a few of these ways. First, bird-dogging and whole-selling are no money-down deals; you don't need any money or credit. But you must be very aggressive!

As an investor you find great deals for other investors and pass the deal on to them for a profit or fee.

Your strategy is the key to your destiny, so that you can survive in this economy.

ALL I WANT TO KNOW, ARE YOU READY TO GROW?

**ALL I WANT TO KNOW,
ARE YOU READY TO GROW?**

Wholesale

- **No Credit / No Money Down**
- **Two Ways to Build an Investor List**
  1. Real Estate Investment Group
  2. Newspaper Ads
- **Net Amount and Location**
- **Find a Deal**
  1. Realtor
  2. Drive By
  3. Newspaper
- **Obtain Contract**
  1. Pre-Qualification Letter
  2. Earnest Money Deposit
  3. Ratified Contract
- **Call Investor Number 2**
- **Establish a Contract Agreement**
- **Payment Received**

ALL I WANT TO KNOW, ARE YOU READY TO GROW?

STREAMS OF INCOME

My people are destroyed for lack of knowledge: because, thou hast rejected knowledge. Hosea 4:6A

REAL ESTATE

<u>Second,</u> there's something called retailing. Retailing is when you buy a piece of property at wholesale, meaning distress or needs repairs, <u>cosmetic</u>, or <u>rehabbing,</u> then resale the property at a retail price, which is the market value. Buy low and sell high. Some call it flipping.

Now let's talk a little, about cosmetic work and rehabbing work.

What are you going to do when your money gets funny and your change gets strange and you're all alone, stuck in the rain?

ALL I WANT TO KNOW, ARE YOU READY TO GROW?

STREAMS OF INCOME

Wealth and riches shall be in his house: and his righteousness endureth for ever. Psalms 112:3

REAL ESTATE

Cosmetic work means changing the carpet, painting, cleaning, changing the kitchen and, bathroom necessities, curb appeal, etc.

Rehabbing work means adding bathrooms, changing roofs, finishing basements, adding walls, adding 2X4's studs, adding 2X12s, joist and drywall etc.

As you can see, cosmetic work is a much smaller job than rehabbing and less costly.

Wealth is not allocated: wealth is created. How long have you waited?

ALL I WANT TO KNOW, ARE YOU READY TO GROW?

STREAMS OF INCOME

I can do all things through Christ which strengtheneth me. Philippians 4:13

REAL ESTATE

You make your money from a retailing deal, as we stated earlier, by selling the property for more than what your expenses would be. Your normal expenses would be: #1 Earnest money deposit, #2 Appraisal Fee, #3 Homeowner Insurance, #4 Closing Costs, #5 Down Payment, #6 Fix-up Cost, and #7 Loan Payments until the house sells. The sales price of the house should exceed all of these expenses. The difference between the sales price and these expenses is your profit.

You must visualize it and realize it to materialize it!

ALL I WANT TO KNOW, ARE YOU READY TO GROW?

Fix Up Cosmetic / Pt. 1

- **Interior Paint**
  1. Color
     - a. Bone or Antique White
     - b. Two Tone
  2. Type
     - a. Flat (Living room, Bedroom)
     - b. Glossy (Bath & Kitchen)

  Estimate - $1000

- **Floors Types**
  1. Hardwood
     - a. Plank
     - b. Parquet
     - c. Hardwood Strip
  2. Carpet
     - a. Bone
     - b. Beige

  Estimate - $1500

ALL I WANT TO KNOW, ARE YOU READY TO GROW?

Fix Up Cosmetic / Pt. 2

- **Kitchens**
  1. Cabinetry
  2. Stoves
  3. Refrigerator
  4. Counter Tops
  5. Linoleum

- **Estimate - $1500**

  Bath
  1. Vanity
  2. Lighting
  3. Tub
  4. Toilet (Wax Ring)

- **Estimate - $500**

ALL I WANT TO KNOW, ARE YOU READY TO GROW?

Fix Up Cosmetic / Pt. 3

- **Curb Appeal**
  1. Yard Items
  - a. Mulch
  - b. Trim Bushes
  - c. White Rocks

- **Door Items**
  1. Hardware
  - a. Locks
  - b. Knocker
  - c. Kick Plate

Miscellaneous
  1. Switches
  2. Sockets
  3. Globes
  4. Vents

- **Labor**

- **Estimate - $2000**

ALL I WANT TO KNOW, ARE YOU READY TO GROW?

Fix Up Rehab / Pt. 1

- **Plumbing**
  1. Water Pipe
     a. Copper (High Cost)
     b. CPVC (Low Cost)
     c. Quest Pipe
     d. Galvanized

  2. Drain Pipe
     a. Cast Iron
     b. PVC

  3. 2-Type Drainage System
     a. Septic Tank
     b. Public Sewage

ALL I WANT TO KNOW, ARE YOU READY TO GROW?

Fix Up Rehab / Pt. 2

- **Drywall**
  1. Material
     - a. 2 X 4 Wood Studs (High Cost)
     - b. 2 X 4 Metal Studs (Low Cost)
  3. 5/8 or ½ inch Drywall
  4. Joint Compound and Tape

- **Frame Up**
  1. Basement Walls
     - a. Treated Lumber or Metal Studs
  2. Bathrooms
     - a. Use Green Board (Steam & Moisture)

- **Roof**
  1. Roof Topping
     - a. Plywood
     - b. Felt
     - c. Shingles

- **Roof Structure**
  1. Studs and Installation

ALL I WANT TO KNOW, ARE YOU READY TO GROW?

STREAMS OF INCOME

REAL ESTATE

<u>Third,</u> would be renting, renting is when a person lives in a home without ownership, meaning they are living in a home but their name is not on the deed or title.

The person staying in the home is called a tenant, and the person who owns that home who is not there is called the landlord. The landlord makes money off the property, by charging the tenant more than his or her expenses meaning the tenant would exceed the landlord's mortgage, insurance, maintenance, and management payments.

If you can conceive it and if you can believe it, then surely you can achieve it. (God will retrieve it!)

ALL I WANT TO KNOW, ARE YOU READY TO GROW?

STREAMS OF INCOME

A good man leaveth an inheritance to his children's children: and the wealth of the sinner is laid up for the just. Proverbs 13:22

REAL ESTATE

The <u>fourth</u> would be foreclosures. A foreclosure is when a homeowner can no longer meet their mortgage payment or financial obligation with the bank.

There are three stages of foreclosure:
1. Pre-foreclosure
2. Foreclosure
3. Post foreclosure

They might knock you down, but they can't knock you out: if you can look up, you can get up: sometimes you might have to shut up to obtain strength, so you can kick butt. L.B./C.G.

ALL I WANT TO KNOW, ARE YOU READY TO GROW?

STREAMS OF INCOME

For what shall it profit a man, if he shall gain the whole world, and lose his own soul? Mark 8:36

REAL ESTATE

Pre-foreclosure *is prior to going into foreclosure. This is when you have time to prevent the foreclosure from occurring. At this point the homeowner is normally three months behind on their mortgage payments and owes penalties and lawyer fees.*

Be humble, so that you don't stumble; then you won't fumble in the game of life!

ALL I WANT TO KNOW, ARE YOU READY TO GROW?

STREAMS OF INCOME

*Train up a child in the way he should go:
and when he is old, he will not depart from it.
Proverbs 22:6*

REAL ESTATE

Foreclosure *is when the homeowner's home is sold at the courthouse. There are several ways for a homeowner to prevent foreclosure:*

Here are a few basic ways:
(1) loan modification
(2) forbearance agreement
(3) short sale
(4) bankruptcy

One man put it best: tough times don't last, but tough people do!

ALL I WANT TO KNOW,
ARE YOU READY TO GROW?

STREAMS OF INCOME

Give, and it shall be given unto you: good measure, pressed down, and shaken together. And running over, shall men give into your bosom. Luke 6:38

REAL ESTATE

Post Foreclosure *is when the home does not sell at the courthouse and goes back to the bank which would now be called an REO (real estate owned by banks).*

You can make money from a foreclosure as a consultant or by doing a short sale.

Motivation and inspiration are great, but until you acquire an interpretation, that allows a transformation, you won't see any elevation.

ALL I WANT TO KNOW, ARE YOU READY TO GROW?

Foreclosure / Pt. 1

- **Major Types of Foreclosure**
  1. VA
  - a. Insured Loan
  - b. Government Funded

  2. HUD
  - a. Insured Loan
  - b. Government Funded
  - c. FHA Loan

  3. REO
  - a. Conventional Loan

- **What Can Stop A Foreclosure**

  1. Loan Modification

  2. Forbearance Agreement

  3. Short Sale
  - a. BPO
  - b. Hardship Letter

- **4. Bankruptcy**

ALL I WANT TO KNOW, ARE YOU READY TO GROW?

Foreclosure / Pt. 2

- **How To Find a Foreclosure**
  1. Banks, Savings and Loans
  2. Private Lenders
  3. Internet
  4. Title companies
  5. Legal newspaper
  6. Courthouse
  7. County, State and Federal agencies

3 Phases of Foreclosure
1. Pre Foreclosure
2. Foreclosure
3. Post Foreclosure

- **Essential Bank Departments**
  1. Payment Department
  2. Collection Department
  3. Litigation Department
  4. REO Department (PF)
     a. Repossession

ALL I WANT TO KNOW, ARE YOU READY TO GROW?

Foreclosure / Pt. 3

- **Foreclosure Strategies**
  1. Foreclosure Consultant
- 2. Buy Owner's Home At Cost

- **Analyzing as an Investor**
  1. Find Out From Title Company if Liens or Encumberson
  2. Find Out Owed Amount on Property
     a. Pay Off Value
  3. Value of Property
  4. Reinstatement Amount
     a. Letter of Release

ALL I WANT TO KNOW, ARE YOU READY TO GROW?

Real Estate

ALL I WANT TO KNOW, ARE YOU READY TO GROW?

STREAMS OF INCOME

Real Estate Notes:

_____

_____

_____

_____

_____

_____

_____

_____

_____

_____

_____

_____

_____

_____

_____

_____

ALL I WANT TO KNOW,
ARE YOU READY TO GROW?

STREAMS OF INCOME

Real Estate Strategies:

_____

_____

_____

_____

_____

_____

_____

_____

_____

_____

_____

_____

_____

_____

_____

_____

ALL I WANT TO KNOW,
ARE YOU READY TO GROW?

STREAMS OF INCOME

Real Estate Actions Taken:

_____

_____

_____

_____

_____

_____

_____

_____

_____

_____

_____

_____

_____

_____

_____

_____

ALL I WANT TO KNOW,
ARE YOU READY TO GROW?

STREAMS OF INCOME

VENDING MACHINES

Income Stream # 2:
The Vending Machine Business

One of the ways to create wealth in America, is to provide a product or service to the American public in volume. It's all about the candy coins and dollar bills which add up to chink, chink, chink.

The vending machine industry is very profitable and simple.

Let's talk about vending machine products.

Remember, your current location is not your final destination! K. M.

ALL I WANT TO KNOW, ARE YOU READY TO GROW?

STREAMS OF INCOME

VENDING MACHINES

Larger candy items; such as candy bars, crackers, potato chips, Lifesavers, and gum generally cost about 85 cents per ven. Your soda machines would be about a dollar per ven. Each time a piece of candy or soda is distributed out of a machine this is called a ven.

Normally, small candy machines, which can house gumballs, peanuts, Chiclets, prizes, etc costs about 25 cents per ven. There are several types of vending machines,

What product or service have you been blessed with, to bring to the marketplace, but because of fear your talent is just a waste?

ALL I WANT TO KNOW, ARE YOU READY TO GROW?

STREAMS OF INCOME

VENDING MACHINES

such as two head machines, three head machines, soda machines, and large candy and potato chip machines.

Let's focus on machine types. #1) Soda machines are very labor intensive, like a job: they are also very heavy, and replenishing of the product can be very often.

Sodas machines are very expensive also. #2) Candy machines are not as labor intensive

Even the best of the best have failed like the rest, but the only difference; they comeback to clean up their mess, that's the test for success!

ALL I WANT TO KNOW,
ARE YOU READY TO GROW?

STREAMS OF INCOME

For we walk by faith, not by sight.
Corinthians 6:7

VENDING MACHINES

as soda machines or as heavy, the kind of candy I'm thinking of are your gumballs, peanuts, Chiclets, prizes, etc. Also, you only replenish candy products on a monthly basis as opposed to a weekly basis with a soda machine which contributes to less labor and time.

Let's focus on profits. Profits can be very rewarding in the vending machine business. You can obtain between 200 percent to 800 percent return on your investments.

Sometimes business can be a mess, but it's nothing but a test: so do your due diligence and preparation and you shall soar above the rest.

ALL I WANT TO KNOW, ARE YOU READY TO GROW?

STREAMS OF INCOME

VENDING MACHINES

From my experiences the gumball machine generates one of the greatest returns on investment. In this industry you must obtain multiple machines to succeed in the vending machine business.

Don't misunderstand me: you can make a good profit from one machine, but it's not going to pay the bills. Distribution is king, meaning whoever has the most distribution points will win. To create wealth you must provide a product or service to the public in volume.

It's time to be motivated, it's time to be stimulated, and it's time to be celebrated.

ALL I WANT TO KNOW, ARE YOU READY TO GROW?

117

STREAMS OF INCOME

VENDING MACHINES

Let's talk about placement. Your machines must be placed not at home in your basement or in your garage: you must hire a company that will place your machines. They are called placement companies, and normally you must have two machines or more to have your machines placed. Vending machines are normally placed in locations, such as: hotels, restaurants, barbershops, hair salons, malls, schools, and government agencies.

In business you can't quit, you can't split, you can't run out on it, you got to be legit, so step up to the plate and get a hit.

ALL I WANT TO KNOW, ARE YOU READY TO GROW?

**ALL I WANT TO KNOW,
ARE YOU READY TO GROW?**

STREAMS OF INCOME

Vending Machine Notes:

_____

_____

_____

_____

_____

_____

_____

_____

_____

_____

_____

_____

_____

_____

_____

_____

_____

_____

ALL I WANT TO KNOW,
ARE YOU READY TO GROW?

STREAMS OF INCOME

Vending Machine Strategies:

_____

_____

_____

_____

_____

_____

_____

_____

_____

_____

_____

_____

_____

_____

_____

_____

ALL I WANT TO KNOW,
ARE YOU READY TO GROW?

STREAMS OF INCOME

Vending Machine Actions Taken:

_____

_____

_____

_____

_____

_____

_____

_____

_____

_____

_____

_____

_____

_____

_____

ALL I WANT TO KNOW,
ARE YOU READY TO GROW?

STREAMS OF INCOME
FINANCIAL PORTFOLIO

Income Stream # 3:
Financial Portfolio

Dealing with Stocks, Bonds, Mutual Funds, Silver, Gold or Commodities!

Stocks

Investing in the stock market can be very profitable or very costly. Understanding the key stocks to buy can be key to your market success.

There are a variety of stocks to choose from. Let's name a few:

> *In life you must take risk, you can either hit or miss. But, until you try, you will never be noticed or on anybody's list!*

ALL I WANT TO KNOW,
ARE YOU READY TO GROW?

STREAMS OF INCOME

In the beginning was the Word, and the Word was with God, and the Word was God. John 1:1

FINANCIAL PORTFOLIO

Income Stocks

Income stocks are stocks that pay a consistent dividend; dividends are just like a small reward a company pays for owning shares of its stock.

The company takes a portion of its earnings which it divides and distributes to its shareholders.

Dividends are a regular income stream. Income stocks not only pay dividends but also provide capitol appreciation.

Every real man has a plan: without a plan, you don't have a leg to stand.

ALL I WANT TO KNOW, ARE YOU READY TO GROW?

STREAMS OF INCOME

FINANCIAL PORTFOLIO

Growth Stocks

Growth stocks are stocks where the owners of the company normally reinvest most of their profits to expand or help the growth of the business, the price of each share of stock will normally grow as the company grows. Stocks may seem complicated but they can be broken down into two basic groups: common stock and preferred stock.

Follow your heart if you want to be successful and not in the dark.

ALL I WANT TO KNOW, ARE YOU READY TO GROW?

STREAMS OF INCOME

FINANCIAL PORTFOLIO

Common Stock

Common stock shareholders share in the success or failure of the company. What happens in the business that year is what happens to your portfolio; sometimes dividends are received. Common stock is the most common form of stock you will encounter. It is easy to trade when the market opens. Common stock shareholders usually have voting rights and have higher potential for return compared to preferred stock holders.

Behind every man or woman's success and glory, there is always one powerful story.

ALL I WANT TO KNOW, ARE YOU READY TO GROW?

STREAMS OF INCOME

FINANCIAL PORTFOLIO

Preferred Stock

Preferred stock not only represents partial ownership of a company like common stock but also pays dividends at specified rates. In addition, dividends are paid to preferred stockholders before common stockholders. Also, if a company is performing poorly, common stockholder's dividends are removed first; moreover, if a company sells its assets because of bankruptcy, preferred stockholders have a claim on the assets before common stockholders.

Great financial skills allow you to pay the bills, without creditors being on your hills.

ALL I WANT TO KNOW, ARE YOU READY TO GROW?

STREAMS OF INCOME

Trust in the Lord with all thine heart; and lean not unto thine own understanding. Proverbs 3:5

FINANCIAL PORTFOLIO

Cyclical Stocks

Cyclical stocks are stocks that increase in value when the economy inclines, and decrease in value when the economy declines. Timing is essential.

You can't go through life, playing it safe on first base and never taking a chance to win the race, to get to home plate!

ALL I WANT TO KNOW, ARE YOU READY TO GROW?

STREAMS OF INCOME

FINANCIAL PORTFOLIO

Defensive Stocks

Defensive stocks are stocks that are used as a defense to maintain some balance when other stocks in your portfolio are not doing so well. These stocks help to maintain the value based on the types of products that are associated with the shares. A product would be something like food and utilities: these kinds of products and services will always be needed no matter what the economy is like.

Freedom is a choice: you have a voice, so stay the course.

ALL I WANT TO KNOW, ARE YOU READY TO GROW?

STREAMS OF INCOME

And Jabez called on the God of Israel, saying, Oh that thou wouldest bless me indeed, and enlarge my coast, and that thine hand might be with me. Chronicles 4:10

FINANCIAL PORTFOLIO

Penny Stocks

Penny stocks are stocks that normally cost less than five dollars per share. These stocks are more affordable for most traders.

Let's talk about blue chip stocks. Blue chip stocks are traded with the bigger companies: they are the usual household names and tend to be the larger mid-cap stocks. Blue chips have a long operating history, steady earnings, and a good reputation and are quite safe to buy.

If you choose the right stocks, you can create wealth, like Fort Knox.

ALL I WANT TO KNOW, ARE YOU READY TO GROW?

STREAMS OF INCOME

In the beginning God created the heavens and the earth.   Genesis 1:1

FINANCIAL PORTFOLIO

Let's talk about the Dow Jones Industrial Average.

The Dow Jones Industrial Average is a large cap index of 30 large company industrial stocks. Dow Jones and Company, Inc. provides worldwide business and financial news and information, through newspapers, newswires magazines, and the Internet; as well as television and radio.

Houses and land you must understand to build wealth and have a family plan.

ALL I WANT TO KNOW, ARE YOU READY TO GROW?

STREAMS OF INCOME

For God hath not given us the spirit of fear; but of power, and of love, and of a sound mind.
2nd Timothy 1:7

The editors of the Wall Street Journal which is owned by Dow Jones and Company, picks the stocks comprised of the Dow Jones Industrial Average, while an SNP committee picks the 500 stocks in the SNP 500.

Pay your bills on time: then creditors don't mine, lending you more than a dollar or dime.

ALL I WANT TO KNOW,
ARE YOU READY TO GROW?

STREAMS OF INCOME

This is the day which the LORD hath made; we will rejoice and be glad in it. Psalm 118:24

FINANCIAL PORTFOLIO

The Dow is comprised of 30 of the largest companies in the US across a range of industries except for transport and utilities. The criteria for a company to get on the Dow Jones voyage, is that the company must be a leader in the industry and very large.

It's time to stop calling Mommy in a bad economy! It's time to rise up a face the reality.

ALL I WANT TO KNOW, ARE YOU READY TO GROW?

STREAMS OF INCOME

Thou oughtest therefore to have put my money to the exchangers, and then at my coming I should have received mine own with usury. Matthew 25:27

FINANCIAL PORTFOLIO

Let's talk about the SNP500 composite. It is an index consisting of 500 stocks chosen for the market size liquidity and Industry grouping among other factors the SNP500 is designed to be a leading indicator of US equities and is meant to reflect the risk return characteristics of the large cap universe. The SNP500 is one of the most commonly used benchmarks for the overall U.S. stock markets.

Now, let's talk about other exciting markets .

God has your back in any economy, don't forget that: you might bend, but you won't crack.

ALL I WANT TO KNOW, ARE YOU READY TO GROW?

STREAMS OF INCOME

Beloved, I wish above all things that thou mayest prosper and be in health, even as thy soul prospereth.
3rd John 1:2

FINANCIAL PORTFOLIO

The American Stock Exchange is the third largest stock exchange by trading volume in the United States. The American Stock Exchange is located in New York City and handles about 10 percent of all securities traded in the United States. A Security Exchange located in downtown Manhattan that is noted for the variety of its listing. Companies with shares traded on the American Stock Exchange are generally smaller than those on the NYSE.

Money, can be sweet like honey, but when your out, it's like a bee sting and it's not funny!

ALL I WANT TO KNOW, ARE YOU READY TO GROW?

STREAMS OF INCOME

Greater love hath no man than this, that a man lay down his life for his friends. St. John 15:13

FINANCIAL PORTFOLIO

Let's talk about the New York Stock Exchange The NYSE is the world's leading and most technologically advanced equity market. A broad spectrum of the market participants including listed companies, individual investors, institutional investors and member firms creates the New York Stock Market. Buyers and seller meet directly in a fair, open and orderly market to access the best possible price through the interplay of supply and demand.

Winner's fight back, loser's never attack!

ALL I WANT TO KNOW, ARE YOU READY TO GROW?

STREAMS OF INCOME

FINANCIAL PORTFOLIO

*Let's talk about NASDAQ. NASDAQ 100
composite also referred to as over the counter,
normally deals with the most aggressive
technology companies.*

Now, let's focus on some stock market terms:

*A man without a strategy is like a man with no
key, locked out of his treasure chest, never to
see what he could truly be!*

ALL I WANT TO KNOW,
ARE YOU READY TO GROW?

STREAMS OF INCOME

FINANCIAL PORTFOLIO

For instance, PE Ratio: many investors are looking for a quick and easy way to determine what stocks to buy. Many Wall Street professionals use the PE ratio or price per earnings ratio. In order to figure out the PE ratio of a stock, take the share price and divide it by the average earnings per share of the past four quarters. You can compare this ratio with the overall market PE.

Now, let's talk about the Most Active Issues. Being broke is like a disease: we must find the cure. And the cure is financial knowledge.

ALL I WANT TO KNOW, ARE YOU READY TO GROW?

STREAMS OF INCOME

FINANCIAL PORTFOLIO

Most Active Issues are normally the most aggressive and active stocks for that time period.

Let's talk a bit about stock splits. Stock splits occur when a public company issues more shares of stock to existing shareholders. Let's focus on IPOs. IPOs are Initial Public Offerings from companies. Let's name a few bonds within the bond market.

Stocks, bonds and mutual funds, can create family wealth if you want some!

ALL I WANT TO KNOW, ARE YOU READY TO GROW?

STREAMS OF INCOME

When I was a child, I spake as a child, I understood as a child, I thought as a child: but when I became man. I put away childish things. Corinthians 13:11

FINANCIAL PORTFOLIO

Municipal Bonds, U.S. Treasury Notes and Bonds, Agency Bonds and Corporate Bonds.

Now, let's focus on Mutual Funds. Mutual Funds are managed by professional money managers. A mutual fund consists of a group of bundled stocks or stocks within one fund.

Men, no romance without finance, no summer fun without income. So, let's get some!

ALL I WANT TO KNOW, ARE YOU READY TO GROW?

Famous American Investor, Stock Market Guru **WARREN BUFFET!**

ALL I WANT TO KNOW, ARE YOU READY TO GROW?

STREAMS OF INCOME

Stock Market Notes:

_____

_____

_____

_____

_____

_____

_____

_____

_____

_____

_____

_____

_____

_____

ALL I WANT TO KNOW,
ARE YOU READY TO GROW?

STREAMS OF INCOME

Stock Market Strategies:

_____

_____

_____

_____

_____

_____

_____

_____

_____

_____

_____

_____

_____

_____

_____

_____

ALL I WANT TO KNOW,
ARE YOU READY TO GROW?

STREAMS OF INCOME

Stock Market Actions Taken:

_____

_____

_____

_____

_____

_____

_____

_____

_____

_____

_____

_____

_____

_____

_____

_____

_____

ALL I WANT TO KNOW,
ARE YOU READY TO GROW?

STREAMS OF INCOME

Income Stream # 4:
Network Marketing

Network marketing, also known as multilevel marketing or MLM. Network marketing is a great business. Network marketing is one of the best ways a product or service can be marketed by word of mouth with great success.

*Network marketing is one of the best industries to prepare a person for entrepreneurship. It is well known for training people to succeed in business. It will equip you with knowledge to overcome your fears of failing in business. You will be conditioned to handle **no-no** until you get a **yes**.*

Learn how to network to increase your net worth!

ALL I WANT TO KNOW, ARE YOU READY TO GROW?

STREAMS OF INCOME

NETWORK MARKETING

This process of conditioning will help to develop the winning attitude and the methodology to excel and be successful in any form of business. There are various titles in network marketing, your title determines your rank and compensation. Here are a few examples of titles: AS is for Associate, RD is for Regional Director, ED stands for Executive Director, PD stands for Presidential Director, diamond, emerald, ruby, and so on and so forth.

Mindset development is critical for your survival on any level!

ALL I WANT TO KNOW, ARE YOU READY TO GROW?

STREAMS OF INCOME

I am Alpha and Omega, the beginning and the ending, saith the Lord, which is and which was, and which is to come the Almighty. Revelations 1:8

NETWORK MARKETING

Have you ever been to a good play or movie and told somebody about it? Did you get paid? Well in networking, the same principles are applied, but you get paid. Prospecting is a very essential component of the business this is the main avenue for building a winning team. There are many ways of prospecting such as; conversing with a friend or relatives, sharing books, tapes, CD's, handouts, third party materials, etc. You must build a group of survivors to have a winning chance.

God wants to get a blessing to you, if he can get one through you! (Bless somebody today!)

ALL I WANT TO KNOW, ARE YOU READY TO GROW?

STREAMS OF INCOME

Brethren, if a man be over taken in a fault, ye which are spiritual, restore such an one in the spirit of meekness; Considering theyself, lest thou also be tempted. Galatians 6:1

NETWORK MARKETING

In my book, "Losing Is Not an Option": "It's not enough hours in a day to create wealth by yourself. So build your team and go full steam, and you will be blessed with your dream." "Remember, some will, some won't, so what. Lets talk about follow-up."

Follow up is one of the key ingredients in order to have great success in network marketing. Many net-workers fail because of the lack of follow-up. This key component can make or break your business.

Before 65, should be your desire to retire!

ALL I WANT TO KNOW, ARE YOU READY TO GROW?

STREAMS OF INCOME

NETWORK MARKETING

Presentations are a very important part of your success in network marketing also: you must learn to do presentations and train your down line to do presentations. Never shotgun your presentations.

There are several types of presentations: lunch, group, conference call, and celebration presentations. Products and compensation plans are very essential to this type of business.

You must study day and night, to get it right, so Mom and Dad won't worry so bad.

ALL I WANT TO KNOW, ARE YOU READY TO GROW?

STREAMS OF INCOME

NETWORK MARKETING

Let's talk about a few compensation plans. One would be the Binary plan; binary means two, meaning you need at least two people in your business to get paid. The next would be the Uni level plan; this is an unlimited plan.

And the final one would be the Break away plan; meaning that your team will eventually break away from your business.

This is my year to grow, I need the cash flow, I want the real DOW because I don't ever want to be poor!

ALL I WANT TO KNOW, ARE YOU READY TO GROW?

STREAMS OF INCOME

So God created man in his own image, in the image of God created he him; male and female created he them. Genesis 1:27

NETWORK MARKETING

Network marketing is one of the best business opportunities that exist where you can build a large business with very little money; as few as a $300.00 startup fee right from your own home with no brick or mortar.

N.M. is a teaching business. One of the keys are to teach your down line or associates how to teach their subordinates how to teach.

Think about the economy, economically, financially, globally, nationally even within your society, maybe in your company. (BAD!)

ALL I WANT TO KNOW, ARE YOU READY TO GROW?

STREAMS OF INCOME

NETWORK MARKETING

New prospects with experience only have two questions; what's your product? And how does your compensation plan work?

In this business you have to be able to believe in your product. It needs to be a consumable product so that the customer will return for repeated business. This puts you in position for residual income, getting paid over and over.

Principle laws, you must sow in order to reap. Will you weep, because you were too cheap?

ALL I WANT TO KNOW, ARE YOU READY TO GROW?

STREAMS OF INCOME

And he said unto him, Well, thou good servant: because thou hast been faithful in a very little, have thou authority over ten cities. Luke 19:17

NETWORK MARKETING

In your business when it comes to recruiting you don't just add and subtract from your business you want to multiply. In network marketing recruiting is the most difficult task for most people; trying to find good business partners to come along and join your team is not easy. In recruiting a good strategy is this: anybody within ten feet of you should hear about your business. A good recruiting technique would be to use third party questions:

Take action or pack it in, use it or lose it!

ALL I WANT TO KNOW, ARE YOU READY TO GROW?

STREAMS OF INCOME

For the LOVE of money is the root of all evil: which while some coveted after, they have erred from the faith, and pierced themselves through with many sorrows.   Timothy 6:10

NETWORK MARKETING

ask your potential recruit if they know someone who might need your product or opportunity, instead of asking them directly.

ALL I WANT TO KNOW,
ARE YOU READY TO GROW?

STREAMS OF INCOME

Network Marketing Notes:

_____

_____

_____

_____

_____

_____

_____

_____

_____

_____

_____

_____

_____

_____

ALL I WANT TO KNOW,
ARE YOU READY TO GROW?

STREAMS OF INCOME

Network Marketing Strategies:

_____

_____

_____

_____

_____

_____

_____

_____

_____

_____

_____

_____

_____

_____

_____

_____

ALL I WANT TO KNOW,
ARE YOU READY TO GROW?

STREAMS OF INCOME

Network Marketing Actions Taken:

_____

_____

_____

_____

_____

_____

_____

_____

_____

_____

_____

_____

_____

_____

_____

_____

ALL I WANT TO KNOW,
ARE YOU READY TO GROW?

STREAMS OF INCOME

Income Stream #5:
The Hotel Industry

It's the shortest because it's the quickest and most power-fullest with the greatest risk, but it can set you free in a hurry based on the astronomical amount of money. The hotel industry is a business system meaning you don't work or operate it, you find someone else to oversee it.

My only enemy is poverty: if I want to be free I must become wealthy for my family and me!

ALL I WANT TO KNOW,
ARE YOU READY TO GROW?

STREAMS OF INCOME

If they obey and serve him, they shall spend their days in prosperity, and their years in pleasures. Job 36:11

HOTEL INDUSTRY

There are two major categories in the hotel industry. One is known as an independent hotel and the next would be a franchise.
Note: With a franchise you will pay a franchise fee and a monthly royalty.

There are essentially three price categories for hotels:
1. The first would be luxury and upscale.
2. The second would be mid market and commercial.
3. The third would be budget and economy .

It's time to make a bold and vertical move!

ALL I WANT TO KNOW, ARE YOU READY TO GROW?

STREAMS OF INCOME

HOTEL INDUSTRY

There are additional classifications of hotels; Motels, Motel Inns, Travel Plazas, Hotel Lodging etc.

There are several major staffing departments in the hotel industry:

1. *Reservation division*
2. *Food and beverage division*
3. *Engineering division*
4. *Housekeeping division*
5. *Accounting division*
6. *Sales division*

Now is the time to bless our youth in mind!

ALL I WANT TO KNOW, ARE YOU READY TO GROW?

STREAMS OF INCOME

The LORD is my light and my salvation; whom shall I fear? The LORD is the strength of my life of whom shall I be afraid? Psalms:27:1

HOTEL INDUSTRY

The key to this strategy is to buy a hotel system that's already operating and running at a 10 percent rate of return on investment and to maintain the same staff and system. There are several types of lending platforms:

1. *Commercial Financing*
2. *SBA Financing*
3. *Seller Financing (Carry Back)*
4. *Hard Money Lenders*
5. *Angel Investors*
6. *Capital Partners*

Hotel, Motel, Holiday Inn; get yourself some Money, and then you can come in!

ALL I WANT TO KNOW, ARE YOU READY TO GROW?

ALL I WANT TO KNOW,
ARE YOU READY TO GROW?

STREAMS OF INCOME

Hotel Notes:

_____

_____

_____

_____

_____

_____

_____

_____

_____

_____

_____

_____

_____

_____

_____

_____

ALL I WANT TO KNOW,
ARE YOU READY TO GROW?

STREAMS OF INCOME

Hotel Strategies:

_____

_____

_____

_____

_____

_____

_____

_____

_____

_____

_____

_____

_____

_____

ALL I WANT TO KNOW,
ARE YOU READY TO GROW?

STREAMS OF INCOME

Hotel Actions Taken:

_____

_____

_____

_____

_____

_____

_____

_____

_____

_____

_____

_____

_____

_____

_____

_____

ALL I WANT TO KNOW,
ARE YOU READY TO GROW?

STREAMS OF INCOME

ATM / MONEY MOVERS (MOST)

Income Stream # 6:
The ATM Money Mover

The ATM industry is a very large business. From city to city, from state to state, from coast to coast, everybody loves to use the most!

It's all about convenience, quick cash when you need it. Automatic teller machines (ATMs) ensure that cash is easily accessible, whenever and wherever someone needs cash. They help businesses facilitate cash-only transactions. And you, avoid mounting credit card fee

> *You must sacrifice and pay the price for a joy filled life.*

ALL I WANT TO KNOW, ARE YOU READY TO GROW?

STREAMS OF INCOME

ATM / MONEY MOVERS (MOST)

processing or check cashing, while also generating revenues for your business via a share of the transaction fees collected by the ATM provider.

Vendors will also install and service your ATM as well as process your transactions, so selecting a vendor that you feel comfortable with is an important step in this process. Make sure the

Meditate and concentrate on your resignation date! (It's time to leave that JOB!)

ALL I WANT TO KNOW, ARE YOU READY TO GROW?

STREAMS OF INCOME

ATM / MONEY MOVERS (MOST)

vendor offers you the best mix of customer service and product quality, and carefully assess the pricing and terms of your agreement. Some vendors may even offer to install the ATM at no cost to your business, and while these agreements can be advantageous, sometimes the fees charged on the backend might be substantially less attractive than those offered elsewhere.

The old strategy doesn't work anymore: go to school, get a good education, get a good job. No more, it's time to create some good jobs!

ALL I WANT TO KNOW, ARE YOU READY TO GROW?

STREAMS OF INCOME

ATM / MONEY MOVERS (MOST)

ATM = Automatic Teller Machine.
There are three (3) basic ways to make money in the ATM industry.

The following ways would be:
  1. *Sell ATM machines as a whole seller. The way to make money as a whole seller, you buy the machines from the manufactures at wholesale prices and sell the machines at retail prices. Your profit is the*

Never hesitate, wait, debate, or you will always be late, for your business date!

ALL I WANT TO KNOW, ARE YOU READY TO GROW?

STREAMS OF INCOME

ATM / MONEY MOVERS (MOST)

difference between the wholesale price
and the retail price. Example: If the
machine cost $2,300 at wholesale and
you sold the machine at retail for $2,700.
Your profit would be $400 per machine.

2. Find companies that could use an ATM
machine at their on site (location). The
way to make money as an ATM bird dog,
is to find businesses that could use the
ATM machine and convince the owner to

Winners never sleep long: losers sleep on and
on.

ALL I WANT TO KNOW,
ARE YOU READY TO GROW?

STREAMS OF INCOME

ATM / MONEY MOVERS (MOST)

buy one. You get paid from making a deal, based on a percentage of each transaction. Example: If each location had about 30 transactions a day and you received 20% of the $2.5 transaction fee. That would be about $150 a day from 10 machines. And the machines are not even yours.

3. *Purchase your own ATM machines or you can lease the machine. The way to make money from owning your own*

Money cometh to you, when you do, what you have been called to do!

ALL I WANT TO KNOW, ARE YOU READY TO GROW?

STREAMS OF INCOME

ATM / MONEY MOVERS (MOST)

machines; would be to find a place with high traffic for your machines. When you own your own machines, you do a lot more work, but you can make a lot more money. You have to supply the machines with the money to get started so you need some cash flow. You need at least $3,000 per machine. You will get it all back, plus a surcharge fee which is your profit. You

In this game called life, when you step onto the field you must carry the ball, or don't play at all. Because in life you must score to get to the successful door.

ALL I WANT TO KNOW, ARE YOU READY TO GROW?

STREAMS OF INCOME

ATM / MONEY MOVERS (MOST)

are in control of the surcharge fee. The surcharge fee could be between $2.00 - $3.50. There are other fee's you need to pay. You must agree to pay the business or location where your machines are placed. The fees are based on the electric and the extra computer phone line that is needed for the machine within, the store-owner's business. Example: Say the store

When will you finish your task and pick up the cash? You can't pick up no funds with the job half done! (Learn how to finish strong!)

ALL I WANT TO KNOW, ARE YOU READY TO GROW?

STREAMS OF INCOME

ATM / MONEY MOVERS (MOST)

*owner gets $1.00 from every $3.00. And with 30 transactions a day, that's $2.00 * 30 equals $60.00 a day. Multiple $60.00 a day times 20 days a month that equals $1,200.00 a month. Multiply 10 machines this equals up to $12,000.00 profit per month.*

Stop being laid back: learn how to be aggressive and attack. It's time to get your money, your house, your car, and your family back!

ALL I WANT TO KNOW, ARE YOU READY TO GROW?

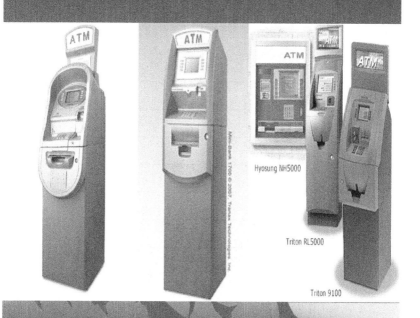

ATM MACHINES
• HYOSUNG, TRANAX & TRITON

Hyosung NH5000

Triton RL5000

Triton 9100

ALL I WANT TO KNOW,
ARE YOU READY TO GROW?

STREAMS OF INCOME

ATM Notes:

_____

_____

_____

_____

_____

_____

_____

_____

_____

_____

_____

_____

_____

_____

_____

ALL I WANT TO KNOW,
ARE YOU READY TO GROW?

STREAMS OF INCOME

ATM Strategies:

_____

_____

_____

_____

_____

_____

_____

_____

_____

_____

_____

_____

_____

_____

_____

_____

_____

ALL I WANT TO KNOW,
ARE YOU READY TO GROW?

STREAMS OF INCOME

ATM Actions Taken:

_____

_____

_____

_____

_____

_____

_____

_____

_____

_____

_____

_____

_____

_____

_____

ALL I WANT TO KNOW,
ARE YOU READY TO GROW?

STREAMS OF INCOME

Create Your Own Stream!
(You can do it!)

Income Stream # 7:
The Million-Dollar Question!

ALL I WANT TO KNOW,
ARE YOU READY TO GROW?

Take Action!

Get started with your very own,
How To Survive In A Bad Economy
Coach Today!

Everyone needs a coach in life.
Working with a coach will help you
to begin a new, successful chapter in
your life. *"Don't waste another
moment."*

Learn how to profit in the good
times <u>and</u> the bad times.

It's time to be the successful person
you were born to be!

_____+++_____

CBS Institute For Learning
*9900-E Greenbelt Rd,
Suite 243
Lanham, MD 20706
Contact Us Today!
Website: www.cbs-wealthbldg.com
Email: cgrant1996@yahoo.com*

_____+++_____

ALL I WANT TO KNOW,
ARE YOU READY TO GROW?

STREAMS OF INCOME

Let's take an example from
Income stream #1: Real Estate

Purchase one piece of property a year for five years at a price of $100,000 each. This could be a condo or a townhome. Purchasing five properties at a $100,000 in five years at this point you will have over $500,000 in assets. By renting these five properties. The rent profits, appreciation (equity build up) on your $500,000 in assets should return around 10 percent return on your investment in a normal year. Which would be $50,000 a year in residual income verses trying to work a job for 40 years obtaining the same results.

It's better to buy than rent, look at all that money spent! Now you still don't have a cent!

ALL I WANT TO KNOW, ARE YOU READY TO GROW?

STREAMS OF INCOME

*Let's take an example from
Income stream # 4: Network Marketing*

*Network marketing is just like a franchise,
such as a McDonald's the only difference a
McDonald's sells hamburgers, fries and
shakes and your franchise sells vitamins,
soap, knowledge, internet products,
e-commerce, etc. Could you imagine
owning your own franchise for less than
$300.00, well it's possible only in Network
marketing where the money you make the
sky is the limit. There is nothing like making
money while you're eating and sleeping.
Take note: in a five year period of time if
you and your team together recruit a total of*

Let your hater's be your motivator.

ALL I WANT TO KNOW,
ARE YOU READY TO GROW?

STREAMS OF INCOME

I am the good shepherd: the good shepherd giveth his life for the sheep. John 10:11

500 people in your down line and if each recruit produce just a $10.00 value to your revenue stream; you will have a residual income of $5,000.00 per month, in a 5 year period of time verses 40 years on a job. Also, note each down-line member of yours is an asset making you money while your in town out of town, even when you're not around. Leaving your job in 5 years should be your motivation, your proclamation, and ultimately your destination.

Always have an attitude of gratitude!

ALL I WANT TO KNOW, ARE YOU READY TO GROW?

YOUTH FINANCIAL PICTURE OF LIFE EXAMPLES!

<u>PATHS:</u>

SCHOOL DROP-OUT
SCHOOL & NO COLLEGE
<u>SCHOOL & COLLEGE</u>

DREAM, YOUNG PEOPLE!

ALL I WANT TO KNOW, ARE YOU READY TO GROW?

Appendix -A

CAREERS AND SALARY EXAMPLES!

SCHOOL DROP OUT (PATH 1)
FIXING HAMBURGERS $16,000 PER YR.
RETAIL CASHIER $18,000 PER YR.

SCHOOL & NO COLLEGE (PATH 2)
SECRETARY $27,000 PER YR
STORE CLERK $30,000 PER YR.
TRUCK DRIVER $35,000 PER YR.

SCHOOL & COLLEGE (PATH 3)
SCHOOL TEACHER $45,000 PER YR.
COMPUTERS $75,000 PER YR.
ENGINEER $100,000 PER YR
DOCTOR OR LAWER $200,000 PER YR.

ALL I WANT TO KNOW, ARE YOU READY TO GROW?

LIFE STYLE EXAMPLE - 1
BASED ON <u>PATH</u> # (1)

$16,000 PAY PER YEAR
$16,000 / 12 MONTH = $1,333   PER MONTH
$1,333 AFTER TAXES, IS $1,066 MONTHLY
<u>MONTHLY REVENUES:</u>
    PAYCHECK (TAKE HOME MONEY) $1,066
<u>MONTHLY EXPENCES:</u>
    TITHES (CHURCH) $ 106
    STAY HOME WITH PARENTS $ 400
    FOOD $ 200
    BUS & CAB $ 260
    CHILDREN $ 100
<u>MONTHLY CASH FLOW</u>   <u>$ 0</u>
    USE FOR INVESTING $ 0
    USE FOR SAVINGS $ 0
    USE FOR (YOU!) $ 0

ALL I WANT TO KNOW, ARE YOU READY TO GROW?

LIFE STYLE EXAMPLE - 2
BASED ON PATH # (1)

$18,000 PAY PER YEAR
$18,000 / 12 MONTHS = $1,500 PER MONTH
$1,500 AFTER TAXES, IS $1,200 MONTHLY
MONTHLY REVENUES:
PAYCHECK (TAKE HOME MONEY) $1,200
MONTHLY EXPENCES:
    TITHES (CHURCH) $ 120
    2 BED RM. / RM. MATE $ 500
    FOOD $ 250
    USED CAR & INS. $ 230
    CHILDREN $ 100
MONTHLY CASH FLOW $ 0
    USE FOR INVESTING $ 0
    USE FOR SAVINGS $ 0
    USE FOR (YOU!) $ 0

ALL I WANT TO KNOW, ARE YOU READY TO GROW?

LIFE STYLE
EXAMPLE - 1
BASED ON <u>PATH</u> # (2)

$27,000 PAY PER YEAR
$27,000 / 12 MONTHS = $2,250   PER MONTH
$2,250 AFTER TAXES, IS $1,800 MONTHLY
<u>MONTHLY REVENUES</u>:
PAYCHECK (TAKE HOME MONEY) $1,800
<u>MONTHLY EXPENCES</u>:
TITHES (CHURCH) $ 180
1 BED APT. & UTILITIES $ 900
FOOD $ 250
CAR & INS. $ 345
CHILDREN $ 100
<u>MONTHLY CASH FLOW</u>   <u>$ 25</u>
USE FOR INVESTING $ 0
USE FOR SAVINGS $ 0
USE FOR (YOU!) $ 25

ALL I WANT TO KNOW,
ARE YOU READY TO GROW?

LIFE STYLE EXAMPLE - 2

BASED ON PATH # (2)

$35,000 PAY PER YEAR
$35,000 / 12 MONTHS = $2,916 PER MONTH
$2,916 AFTER TAXES, IS $2,333 MONTHLY
MONTHLY REVENUES:
PAYCHECK (TAKE HOME MONEY) $2,333
MONTHLY EXPENCES:

TITHES (CHURCH)	$ 233
2 BED CONDO UTILITIES	$1,300
FOOD	$ 300
CAR & INS	$ 250
CHILDREN	$ 100
MONTHLY CASH FLOW	$ 100
USE FOR INVESTING	$ 37.5
USE FOR SAVINGS	$ 37.5
USE FOR (YOU!)	$ 25

ALL I WANT TO KNOW, ARE YOU READY TO GROW?

LIFE STYLE
EXAMPLE - 1
BASED ON PATH # (3)

$75,000 PAY PER YEAR
$75,000 / 12 MONTHS = $6,250   PER MONTH
$6,250 AFTER TAXES, IS $5,000 MONTHLY
MONTHLY REVENUES:
PAYCHECK (TAKE HOME MONEY) $5,000
MONTHLY EXPENCES:

TITHES (CHURCH)	$ 500
MORTGAGE & UTILITIES	$ 2,300
FOOD	$ 400
CAR & INS.	$ 500
CHILDREN	$ 500
MONTHLY CASH FLOW	$ 800
USE FOR INVESTING	$ 500 10%
USE FOR SAVINGS	$ 100
USE FOR (YOU!)	$ 200

ALL I WANT TO KNOW,
ARE YOU READY TO GROW?

LIFE STYLE EXAMPLE - 2
BASED ON <u>PATH</u> # (3)

$200,000 PAY PER YEAR
$200,000 /12 MONTHS = $16,666 PER MONTH
$16,666 AFTER TAXES, IS $13,333 MONTHLY
<u>MONTHLY REVENUES:</u>
PAYCHECK (TAKE HOME) $13,333
<u>MONTHLY EXPENCES:</u>
TITHES (CHURCH) $1,333
MORTGAGE & UTILITIES $4,500
FOOD $ 800
CAR & INS. $1,000
CHILDREN $1,000
<u>MONTHLY CASH FLOW</u>   <u>$4,700</u>
USE FOR INVESTING $2,666   20%
USE FOR SAVINGS $1,000
USE FOR (YOU!) $1,034

ALL I WANT TO KNOW, ARE YOU READY TO GROW?

Always be in the spirit of Inspiration Expectation Anticipation Acceleration Then you can set aside time for celebration!

ALL I WANT TO KNOW, ARE YOU READY TO GROW?

TF = TF

TOTAL

FOCUS

EQUALS

TOTAL

FREEDOM!

ALL I WANT TO KNOW,
ARE YOU READY TO GROW?

<u>DREAMS mean</u>…!

D-Daring
R-Remarkable
E-Everlasting
A-Amazing
M-Magical
S-Successful

**ALL I WANT TO KNOW,
ARE YOU READY TO GROW?**

Five P's

- **Purpose**

- **Passion**

- **Product**

- **Process**

- **Profit**

ALL I WANT TO KNOW, ARE YOU READY TO GROW?

Five P's

- Proper

- Preparation

- Prevents

- Poor

- Performance

ALL I WANT TO KNOW, ARE YOU READY TO GROW?

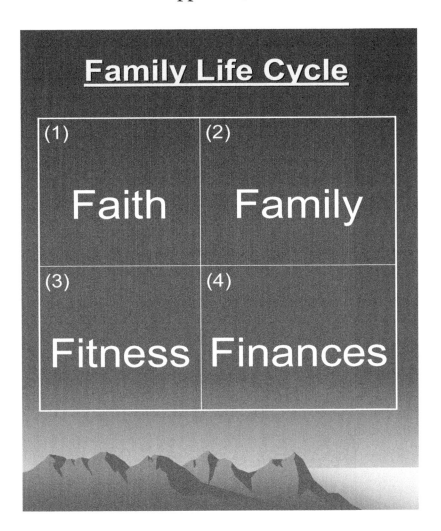

**ALL I WANT TO KNOW,
ARE YOU READY TO GROW?**

4 F's
This is called the Family Life Cycle

FAITH

FAMILY

FITNESS

FINANCES

Focus on these four elements and you will have a balanced life! Follow the sequence from left to right.

ALL I WANT TO KNOW, ARE YOU READY TO GROW?

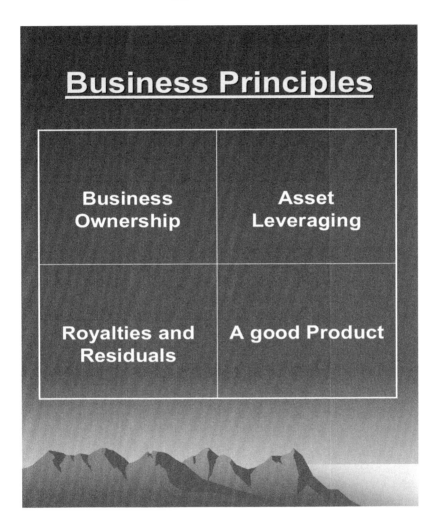

ALL I WANT TO KNOW,
ARE YOU READY TO GROW?

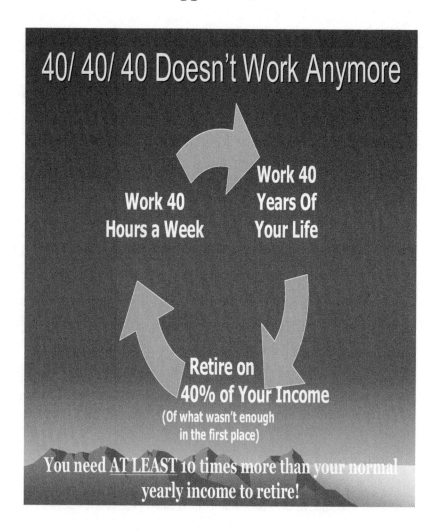

**ALL I WANT TO KNOW,
ARE YOU READY TO GROW?**

Job Loss Solutions

Start your own company today !
If you choose to continue to work a job, follow the advice below:

Steps to take!!!

1. Query the Yellow Pages or Map Quest on line, for the job industry you are looking for and write down the names and numbers of 100 companies.

Call the operator and find out the manager's name and the department and mail your resume directly to them.
Use a red or purple envelope

ALL I WANT TO KNOW, ARE YOU READY TO GROW?

Job Loss Solutions

only with a bow and a thank you card along with your resume inside. This will get your resume noticed. If this does not work go to the company and make the delivery yourself. But, this time you must use a large yellow envelope. I have a package for John Dow, (Your Resume!) or take it to the mail room. Do not dress up, play the part! It's time to be humble.

2. Find out about trade shows in your field and do some research on the show to find out, some of the major players or major companies that are involved. Get their contact info.

ALL I WANT TO KNOW, ARE YOU READY TO GROW?

Job Loss Solutions

3. Send out 50 resumes a week or more, an average of 10 a day.

Look at resume books and search online for top resumes in your field.

Develop 2 – 3 different types of resumes based on what you are applying for.

Fill out 5 online applications a day, 25 a week.

Make 25 phone calls a day. Some of these calls will be to new companies and some will be follow up calls.

ALL I WANT TO KNOW, ARE YOU READY TO GROW?

Job Loss Solutions

4. Practice, practice, practice on your interviewing skills! Always prepare to have three interviews for each company that contacts you.

Try to find out something about the department or the people on the team you're applying for.

So when you get to the interview you can develop a conversation about that topic to build a relationship. This might give you the slight edge you need, which the other interviewers want have.

ALL I WANT TO KNOW, ARE YOU READY TO GROW?

Job Loss Solutions

5. Follow-up is critical, keep track of all names, numbers and emails.

6. Find out the department head's email address, not, the email address in the ad. Then send your resume to the department head's email.

7. The next job you obtain, never put more than one box of stuff in your office, because, when it's time to leave you only want to take one trip out the door and never look back.

ALL I WANT TO KNOW, ARE YOU READY TO GROW?

Job Loss Solutions

Keep your family pictures at home. Stop letting people know all your business. They will find ways to hurt you. Only put pictures up of your mansion, mobile home, and your yacht.

This will keep the focus off your family.

8. Dress for success, like you are the CEO. Men where is your power tie? Women no flat heeled shoes on interviews.

ALL I WANT TO KNOW, ARE YOU READY TO GROW?

Job Loss Solutions

9. Always prep your references; make sure they can speak well and that they will say great things about you. Don't assume or wait to the last moment.

10. Email blast, Twitter, Facebook, MySpace, and call everybody you know and ask who knows about a position that will fit your skill set.

11. Do your homework: go onto the company's website. And learn what type of product or services they

ALL I WANT TO KNOW, ARE YOU READY TO GROW?

Job Loss Solutions

provide. Study their financial statements such as income statements, balance sheets and budget statements.

If you study this material, you should be well versed on the company and be able to impress them and share how you could be an asset and increase their bottom line. You must realize that <u>cash</u> is <u>king</u> in a bad economy!

12. Call your old company, to see if they could still use your services but this time as a consultant. $$$

ALL I WANT TO KNOW, ARE YOU READY TO GROW?

Job Loss Solutions

13. Find five aggressive head-hunters (job seekers!) ASAP!

14. When going to a job fair, always get there at least one hour early, while the company is setting up, and establish a relationship with the staff before everyone gets there. Give them your resume and get their business card, office location, web-site and title. Follow up within 48 hours.

15. Create an email address with the same name as your job title.

ALL I WANT TO KNOW, ARE YOU READY TO GROW?

Appendix D
Products

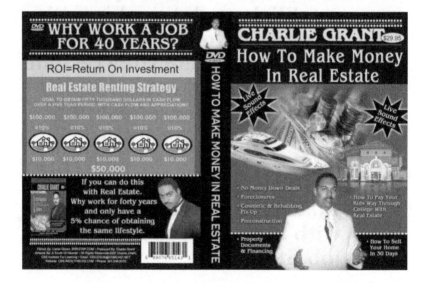

ALL I WANT TO KNOW, ARE YOU READY TO GROW?

Appendix D
Products

ALL I WANT TO KNOW, ARE YOU READY TO GROW?

Appendix D
Products

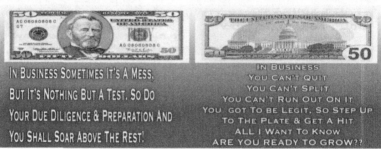

ALL I WANT TO KNOW, ARE YOU READY TO GROW?

Appendix D

Products

*Try Our Economic Empowerment Training,
Learn 7 Different Streams Of Income!
Your Life Won't, Be The Same!*

(*Powerful: speaker's, trainer's, and author's*)
www.cbs-wealthbldg.com

ALL I WANT TO KNOW,
ARE YOU READY TO GROW?

Appendix D
Products

HOMEBASE BUSINESS PRODUCTS

www.cbs-wealthbldg.com

If you, your family,
association, organization, club,
need any training,
e-mail: cgrant1996@yahoo.com
www.cbs-wealthbldg.com

Speakers and coaching also available!

ALL I WANT TO KNOW,
ARE YOU READY TO GROW?

Take Action.

Get started with your very own, *How To Survive In A Bad Economy* Coach Today!

Everyone needs a coach in life. Working with a coach will help you to begin a new, successful chapter in your life. *"Don't waste another moment."*

Learn how to profit in the good times <u>and</u> the bad times.

It's time to be the successful person you were born to be!

_____+++_____

CBS Institute For Learning
9900-E Greenbelt Rd,
Suite 243
Lanham, MD 20706
Contact Us Today!
Website: www.cbs-wealthbldg.com
Email: cgrant1996@yahoo.com

_____+++_____

ALL I WANT TO KNOW, ARE YOU READY TO GROW?

BIO

CEO and FOUNDER CHARLIE GRANT. Born and raised in Washington, DC. He started his career as a computer programmer, then worked as a senior systems analyst. He worked for numerous fortune 500 companies such as: EDS (Electronic Data Systems), Perot Systems, UNIX's, MCI, Freddie Mac, USAir, Marriott, etc. Soon thereafter he founded CBS (COMPUTER BUSINESS SOLUTIONS INC.). After earning a six figure income for several years in computer science, he developed a burning desire to help people, along with a passion to motivate and educate. He noticed a calling on his life. He dropped everything and stepped out on faith to pursue what the LORD had purposed him to do, and the rest is history. Over the last ten years he has inspired, motivated, and educated more than a 100,000 men, women, boys and girls on how to build income producing "assets" through multiple streams of income.

He is a very powerful and gifted Professional Speaker, Author, and Coach. His way of giving back, was to start a FREE Youth program about 4 years ago called YEP (Young Entrepreneurship Program). He continues to speak and train on entrepreneurship and youth empowerment! He has been on many Radio and TV Shows. His very own TV Show was launched, December 1st 2009; called [How To Survive In A Bad Economy].

ALL I WANT TO KNOW, ARE YOU READY TO GROW?

Made in the USA
Middletown, DE
10 April 2023

28413495R00126